SCAMS

SCAMS

Eugene Rooney

Library of Congress Control Number:		2010919380
ISBN:	Hardcover	978-1-4568-4285-7
	Softcover	978-1-4568-4284-0
	Ebook	978-1-4568-4286-4

This book was printed in the United States of America.

To order additional copies of this book, contact:
Xlibris Corporation
1-888-795-4274
www.Xlibris.com
Orders@Xlibris.com
91854

Contents

Introduction

The purpose of this book is to describe the latest scams going on the Internet today and how to avoid some of these scams which have been going on for years. The book will consist of the different types of scams, by chapters, examples of scams tried successfully on me and others not successful that still continue on the Internet today.

The biggest scammers in the past and still today are Nigerians. Russians and Eastern Europeans are not far behind now, and I will also add South Africans.

Nigerians have been scamming since the Internet became worldwide. I think all Nigerians have a PhD in psychology and are the number one in scamming techniques which are done in stages for you to keep sending money. Scamming is part of their culture no matter the educational level. There was a front-page column in the *Wall Street Journal* about Nigerians scamming about twenty years ago.

Once in a while you will see a news report of the Nigerian government raiding computer centers "arresting" scammers, trying to improve their world image, but scanning still goes on today, and Nigeria is listed as one of the most corrupt countries in the world. With the technology in copying and printing, documents that can look "very" official. Be prepared, once you answer a scam, your e-mail address will be passed around.

The types of scams are as follows:

Chapter One

Latest Scams

What is the most despicable latest scam is a CNN news report of a lady shaving her head and eyebrows telling her relatives and friends she needed money for cancer treatments.

Since my late wife looked like this on chemo before she died, I know what a person looks like when going through chemo.

One relative mortgaged their house to give her money and is having problems keeping their house now. They come to find out she had a gambling problem and gambled away three hundred thousand dollars given to her by friends and relatives. A person with a gambling problem truly believes that they are close to the next big win. To fake a serious illness like this, you have no conscience. CNN did not say the results of this despicable scam.

Scammers are using photos of American service men in Iraq and Afghanistan. The service men are asking for help and for you to send money. These service men do not know their photos are being used for this scam. The most vulnerable to this scam are single women seriously wanting to help or searching for companionship and love.

Chapter Two

Lottery

"You have just won 15 million British pounds in our world lottery from your e-mail address." What is interesting about this scam is it is against the law to receive any money from a foreign lottery according to the US Postal Service which I found out recently. To respond to this scam, you are asked your name, address, age, sex, and occupation. All this information is not needed to receive your money or asking for a *fee* to receive your money.

What is interesting about this scam is that the e-mail address of the sender is usually from the UK, which is Great Britain, but this lottery scam is from Belgium. Nigerians live in different countries, not in the US to be prosecuted. My Nigerian scammer lived in Canada.

Chapter Three

Searching for Love

There are some sites that are real in finding a partner on the Internet and is very popular due to our lifestyle today to meet a partner. *But* some of the women give a US address on real sites when they are actually living in a foreign country.

The lady told me she was tired of not meeting the "right" man in Houston, Texas. She told me that she had to go to Benin, Africa from Houston, Texas, and sell her plantation left to her from her father's estate. She had a Korean buyer and would receive over a million USD and not for me to worry about money in the future for our life together. Stage one, she asked for money for a layover in Nigeria for a hotel room on her way back to the US with her money shipped in a sealed case. Stage two, since her sealed case was x-rayed at the airport and cash was discovered in the case, she asked for money to clear customs in Belgium. All bags are x-rayed now at any airport for terrorist bombs. I asked her why she did not deposit the money in an American bank in Benin and have the money wired to the US. She told me there was no American bank like CHASE in Benin. I did not believe there was no American bank in Benin.

She wanted me to pay for the shipping charges to the US, and I refused.

One of my favorite scams is the woman telling you she is from the US but is in Africa on a "buying trip", needs funds to return to the USA.

Another woman from a church, volunteers to bring medicine and food to the poor in Africa, but she needs funds to return to the USA. She states she was robbed or did not bring enough money to return to the US.

Sometimes you will receive photos of beautiful women with children that are in Africa and need funds to return to the USA.

Another love scam is if you send $ 2,500, she will see you in a week—not possible today with Homeland Security requirements.

Of course both are not real. I am a world traveler, and I know that usually you buy a round-trip ticket for approximately twelve hundred to fifteen hundred dollars. A round-trip ticket is always cheaper than one way. Plus US immigration does not give a person a visa in one week, and now you need a passport to travel to the US. The person needs to make an appointment for an interview at the closest embassy/consulate for any visa and especially a tourist visa which can take months. There are changes in Homeland Security since 9/11. Today, the person needs a return-trip ticket from the country they are coming from. Years ago before 9/11, you could enter the US on a one-way ticket promising to show up for an immigration hearing, which many never happen. Today because of 9/11, one-way tickets are very suspicious with Homeland Security and are not allowed coming from a foreign country.

Love is blind? Most of these love scams are on older men believing that a much younger woman is truly interested in a love relationship with him and promises to marry him. For a real marriage to take place, you need photos, actual proof, you meet this person for a future marriage. Also, after coming to the US on a visa, you *must* have a *legal* US marriage within ninety days. US immigration only recognizes US legal marriages, not marriages in a foreign country.

Case in point: A man in his late fifties received merchandise bought with stolen credit cards. The merchandise was shipped to him without him knowing that the items were bought with stolen credit cards. He was repackaging the items and shipping it to different countries. He paid the shipping charges and was promised to be paid back for shipping. He spent thousands and thousands of dollars and never received any payments. This never happened after receiving e-mails promising to pay him for shipping. He found out later, "the beautiful young woman" behind the computer was a Nigerian man living in Switzerland running this scam. Today it is very easy to copy a photo from the Internet of someone else without the person knowing he or she is being used in a scam.

My example: I answered an ad on a well-known "love" site. A woman was telling me, "I am thirty years old and I am tired living alone and almost finished nursing school." Her address was from California.

After writing her an e-mail letter, I received an answer. She was born in the US but moved back to Africa with her African mother after her US-born father died.

I wrote her that I do not send money to Africa. She said she was living in California. I wrote her another e-mail telling her that it was very clear in her last letter she was living in Africa. Never heard from her again.

Another scam was I met this woman on a well-known US Web site. She told me she needed a benefactor before she could get her money from Great Britain. Her address was in Myrtle Beach, South Carolina. She needed money to pay the "tax" to the British government. Her benefactor was a New York politician representing a New York district. With his official Web site, I was sent official-looking documents, death certificate of the father, documents agreeing to be her legal partner. The money had to be sent to a "lawyer" in South Carolina where she was staying. The American, New York, politician "supposed" pay her way to England according to her e-mail to settle her father's estate. However, now I believed she was really living in England from the last photos she sent me. I know what the English countryside looks like because I lived there three years while in the US military. After paying her "legal" fees sent to South Carolina, I received an e-mail to receive monies, we would meet in New York. Of course, I had to pay airfare for her and the

English banker to release the monies from an English bank. This was over two thousand dollars. I refused and asked for my money back from this crooked New York politician. I have been trying for over a year trying to get my money back. I should have known better than sending money to a third party and knowing that the politician had another e-mail address, *not* his New York official public Web site.

Several times I was sent photos of beautiful naked ladies promising me if I sent them gas money they will come to Houston, Texas. One lady sent me an e-mail and said she was in Georgia and needed money for a motel but did not have identification to pick up the money in Georgia. In reality she was still in New York trying to scam me, not in Georgia to pick up money.

Chapter Four

Be My Company Representative, Be a Secret Shopper

Be My Company Representative

This is an actual scam tried on me. I received one a week now. I will go step by step on how this scam works. I answered over several years ago to be a "company representative" for a Japanese company. I was studying Japanese at this time and would write something in Japanese but never receive an answer in Japanese. The standard fee for this scam is you will keep 10 percent of the money collected and wire the rest to the company. Know that it really takes ten days for any check to clear, not five days. I received a check for one hundred fifty thousand dollars from a New York bank, and I asked my bank if it was a bogus check.

I received a call from Canada after I received the check. I knew right away the person talking to me had a Nigerian English accent. After I sent an Excel sheet with the breakdown of charges to wire the money and his share, I asked him where to send the money. He gave me a Hong Kong address. This was the last stage of this scam. I was already suspicious from his phone call from Canada with a Nigerian English accent. My bank informed me that the "official" looking check from a New York bank was not from their bank and was bogus. Why would a Japanese company have money wired to a Hong Kong account? What you are supposed to do is after you deposit the check, you wire the money. When you find out the check is not good, you already wired the money, and you are responsible for this phony check. This scam cost me five dollars for a return check fee from my bank. A legitimate company selling in the US can always wire the money to the home company and does not need me to do this.

After this attempted scam, I received an "official" United Nation documents informing me that the UN will help me get my scam money returned, but it will cost me a fee. Again the UN documents are very "official" looking. This is another scam. The technology to copy "official" looking documents is amazing today.

Be a Secret Shopper

I filled out the form to be a mystery shopper and received a check. When I brought the check to my bank manager and showed it to him, he told me he received many of these checks and are all not real.

Chapter Five

Be My Partner to Share My Millions

I receive this type of scam daily. "I need a partner to share a deceased account before my bank takes over this inactive account. My bank does not know I am doing this and must keep this confidential." Or the owner of this account died with his family and you will claim that you are the closest relative. There seems to be a common scenario to these scams. It appears everyone that dies in these scams dies from a plane crash, but never about a family dying in an auto accident. I believe that in the US forty thousand Americans die each year in auto accidents. Maybe in these scammers' counties there are not many cars for accidents?

Another common scam is using "God and with your help" to share my millions. Using God, these scammers believe that the US is mostly Christians and you will help them. By believing in God you will help them.

To receive these millions you must pay a fee, and this "fee" is the scam.

Chapter Six

Identify and Avoid a Scam

Why are Americans easy to scam? This is because many Americans do not understand the American banking system, especially wiring money; and many have never been out of the US, many from even the state they live in.

These are rules you should follow and know:

It takes at least *ten* days for a check, cashier's check, to clear the bank reserve clearing house. Scammers know this. Banks will cash them and hold you responsible if they are bogus. The company representative is an example of why scammers want you to send the money as soon as possible.

Never accept overpayment for merchandising if you are selling on a listed site where you are asked to send the difference back because the check you receive will not be real.

Never wire by Western Union or MoneyGram, especially to a *third* party, like what happened to me.

Never give out personal financial information—bank account number and social security number. I receive e-mails asking me to reinstate my AOL account that I had for over nineteen years. This is *not* an e-mail from AOL. It is a scam for your credit card number.

Look at the e-mail address. Gmail and Yahoo are common e-mail addresses used by scammers; and they are using foreign countries as an e-mail address, UK (Great Britain), RU (Russia), and HK (Hong Kong).

Look at the time you received the e-mail. You will receive e-mails from Nigerian scammers early in the morning due to the time difference between Africa and US, usually around 3:00 a.m. Most Americans are in bed at this time, not up to write e-mails.

Nigerian scammers have very poor English grammar, using key words such as *soonest* for *soon* and *hear* for *here*. Sometimes the grammar is so poor you will not understand some of the letters. Another clue a foreigner writing you is he or she will put the adjective following the noun. This is proper in their native language—Spanish, Japanese, Vietnamese, etc.—plus using *i* for *I*, not knowing proper English grammar.

Never open an e-mail address when it is attached to the original e-mail. This will be a scam and may have a "worm" attached. There is a "worm" attached to this e-mail.

Remember scammers are after your money, and there are usually three stages for you to keep on sending money with them making all kinds of promises.

I hope after you buy and read this book, you will save hundreds or thousands of dollars in being scammed. This book is not expensive, so you can save you your money.

Remember, scammers want *only* your money, not your love; and most older Americans are very trusting and easy to scam because most do not understand the American banking system, especially wiring money.

Subj: **Immediate opportunity**
Date: 12/24/2010 7:47:16 P.M. Central Standard Time
From: info@pacificemail.net
To: vicmanjlry@aol.com

View images here | Stop receiving these messages here

NEEDED: Motivated Individuals for

Work-at-Home Opportunities Paying up to $87/hr

- No experience needed
- No set hours
- Work part-time or full-time

Get started today — start making money.

CLICK HERE ▶

Saturday, December 25, 2010 AOL: vicmanjlry

http://www.craigslist.org/about/scams

Subj: **Thank You and Be Blessed**
Date: 12/14/2010 6:31:21 A.M. Central Standard Time
From: jjwilma689@aol.com
Reply-to: barrscottdaniel@sbcglobal.net

Hello Friend,

I am Mrs Janie Hammond, I am a US citizen, 59 years Old. I reside here in cook road portland tn. My residential address is as follows.356 cook road portland tn 37148, United States, am thinking of relocating since I am now rich. I am one of those that took part in the Compensation in U.K LONDON many years ago and they refused to pay me, I had paid over $35,000 while in the US, trying to get my payment all to no avail.

So I decided to travel down to U.K LONDON with all my compensation documents, And I was directed to meet Barrister Scott Daniel, who is the member of COMPENSATION AWARD COMMITTEE, and I contacted him and he explained everything to me. He said whoever is contacting us through emails are fake. He took me to the paying bank for the claim of my Compensation payment. Right now I am the most happiest woman on earth because I have received my compensation funds of $1,500,000.00 Moreover, Barrister Scott Daniel showed me the full information of those that are yet to receive their payments and I saw your name as one of the beneficiaries, and your email address, that is why I decided to email you to stop dealing with those people, they are not with your fund, they are only making money out of you.. I will advise you to contact Barrister Scott Daniel.

You have to contact him directly on this information below.

JOAKIN COMPENSATION HOUSE
Name : Barrister Scott Daniel
Email: barrscottdaniel@sbcglobal.net
Phone: +44 70457 24625

You really have to stop dealing with those people that are contacting you and telling you that your fund is with them, it is not in anyway with them, they are only taking advantage of you and they will dry you up until you have nothing. The only money I paid after I met Barrister Scott Daniel was just 150Great Britain Pounds for the paper works, take note of that.

As soon as you contact him he will send you the payment information which you are to use in sending the payment to him in order for him to obtain the document from the court of law there in UK. LONDON so that your fund can be transfer to you without any delay just the way mine was being transfer to me.

Send him the following details if you know you are ready to make the payment so that as soon as he receive your information he will send to you the payment details for sending him the 150Great Britain Pounds that is needed for him to get the document that is needed to make the transfer a successful one without any further payment.

Fill Out the information to him if you are ready to get your fund and also ready to make the payment.

Your Full Name:...............
Direct Phone:....................
Country.................
Occupation:.....................
Gender:.........
Age:.............

Tuesday, December 14, 2010 AOL: vicmanjlry

Once again stop contacting those people, I will advise you to contact Barrister Scott Daniel so that he can help you to Deliver your fund instead of dealing with those liars that will be turning you around asking for different kind of money to complete your transaction.

Thank You and Be Blessed.

Mrs Janie Hammond.
356 cook road portland tn 37148,
United States

Subj.   **HIS EMAIL IS FROM THE UNITED NATION..**
Date: 12/27/2010 2:18:16 P.M. Central Standard Time
From: demo@xlprovider.com
Reply-to: fidelitywilson@rediffmail.com
Attention:

How are you today? Hope all is well with you and family? You may not understand why this email came to you. We have been having a meeting for the passed 7 months which ended 2 days ago with the then secretary to the UNITED NATIONS.

This email is to all the people that have been scammed in any part of the world, the UNITED NATIONS have agreed to compensate them with the sum of USD $850,000 (Eight hundred and fifty thousand United State Dollars Only), This also includes every foreign contractors that may have not received their contract sum, and people that have had an unfinished transaction or international businesses that failed due to Government problems etc.

We found your name in our list and that is why we are contacting you, this has been agreed upon and have been signed.

You are advised to contact Rev. Fidelity Wilson of SPRING TRUST BANK PLC, as he is our representative in Nigeria, contact him immediately for your payment of USD$850,000 (Eight hundred and fifty thousand United State Dollars Only)which way you need the fund to be delivered. So he will send it to you and you can clear it in any bank of your choice.

You are advice to get in contact with Rev. Fidelity Willson and provide him with below information.

Full Name:................................
Address:................................
Telephone Number:............................

Person to Contact Rev. Fidelity Willson
Email: cusomercare-stb@secretarias.com
Tel: +2348080260723

Thanks and God bless you and your family.

Hoping to hear from you as soon as you cash your Fund.

Making the world a better place.

Regards,
Mr. Ban Ki-Moon

Monday, December 27, 2010 AOL: vicmanjlry

Subj: **FINAL RELEASE OF YOUR INHERITANCE FUND**
Date: 12/14/2010 7:35:57 A.M. Central Standard Time
From: fighterz-----1436@att.net
Reply-to: ununitednationss723@gmail.com

YOUR PAYMENT NOTIFICATION
INTERNATIONAL MONETARY FUND (IMF)
HEAD OFFICE NO: 23 AVEILON ROAD,
Lagos State Nigeria.

INSTRUCTION TO RELEASE YOUR INHERITANCE FUND

This office write to inform you that the procedure to release your over due Inheritance
Fund to be paid to you without all those problems that you have been passing through
from (Bank, and courier, company, Diplomat) the IMF AND UNITED NATIONS have
come to redeem you from all the difficulties you have been experiencing in getting your
long over due payment due to excessive demand for money from you by both corrupt
Bank officials and Courier Companies after which your fund remain unpaid to you.

All Governmental and Non-Governmental parasites, NGOs, Finance Companies,
Banks, Security Companies and Courier companies which have been in contact with
you of late have been instructed to back up from your transaction and you have been
advised NOT to respond to them anymore since the IMF AND UNITED NATIONS is
now directly in charge of your payment.

You are hereby advised NOT to remit further payment to any institutions with respect to
your transaction as your fund will be transferred to you directly from our source. I hope
this is clear. Any action contrary to these instructions is at your own risk.

Further more, you are advice to send us your option to avoid mistake and notify me with
your choice of option as stated below for immediate proceed on your transaction.
However, have it known that this morning i have forwarded your information to the
Board of Presidency Federal Republic of Nigeria/Federal Ministry of Finance for final
release and Approval of your over due contract payment. I will get back you as soon as i
receive the payment order from the Board of Presidency.

Obviously, you are advice to use this medium to choose your payment option as stated
below

Payment Option(mode of payment)

Online transfer: You will have to open a new Bank account here and it will be registered
for international transfer and you can make an online transfer as it will take 24Hours to
get the account done.

Tuesday, December 14, 2010 AOL: vicmanjlry

As a matter of fact, you are required to Deal and Communicate only with Mr. AKINSOLA AKINFEMIWA, DIRECTOR INTERNATIONAL REMITTANCE SKYE BANK NIGERIA PLC, with the help and monitory team from the FEDERAL RESERVE BANK OF NEW YORK which is our official remmitting bank, Committee On Foreign Payment Matters in United Nation, has look up to make sure you receive your fund valued $32million. So contact: Mr.AKINSOLA AKINFEMIWA on his contact information,Direct SKYE BANK NIGERIA PLC Email:skyebankplc000002@gmail.com for immediate release of your contract/inheritance/Award Winning claim Be informed that you are not allowed to correspond with | any person or office anymore, You are required to send bellow information for your bank online Transfer.

1) YOUR FULL NAME:
2) ADDRESS,CITY,STATE AND COUNTRY:
3) PHONE,FAX AND MOBILE:
4) COMPANY NAME(IF ANY) POSITION AND ADDRESS:
5) COPY OF YOUR INT'L PASSPORT/DRIVERS LICENSE:

NOTE THAT MY DUTY IS TO HELP MONITOR YOUR TRANSFER AND ONCE I HELP YOU GET YOUR OVER DUE PAYMENT SUM OF $32,000,000 YOU ARE TO PAY ME THE SUM OF $40,000 THAT IS AFTER YOU HAVE RECEIVE THE $32,000,000 IS WHEN YOU PAY FOR THE MONITORING DUTY FEE OF $40,000.

I HOPE THIS IS CLEAR TO YOU?

Await to hear from you as soon as possible with your option and as stated below and call me immediately for more clarification regarding your transaction:

Mr. BAN KI-MOON
UNITED NATIONS SECRETARY GENERAL
Email:ununitednationss723@gmail.com

Tuesday, December 14, 2010 AOL: vicmanjlry

Actual scam emails sent to craigslist users:

Hi,
I am selling this car because my platoon has been sent back to Afganistan and don't want it get old in my backyard. The price is low because I need to sell it before November 16th. It has no damage, no scratches or dents, no hidden defects. It is in immaculate condition, meticulously maintained and hasn't been involved in any accident...I do have the title , clear, under my name. The Denali has 35,000 miles VIN# 1GKEK63U16J138428 .
It is still available for sale if interested, price as stated in the ad $4,300. The car is in Baltimore, MD, in case it gets sold I will take care of shipping. Let me know if you are interested, email back.
Regards!!!

First of all I want to thank you for your interest for my car. I sell it at this price($2,980.00) because I have been divorced recently. Now the car is in my property and as a woman i don't need it. This car is in excellent working conditions, no scratches, flaws or any kind of damage, slightly used in 100% working and looking conditions and comes with a clear title.

From the beginning you have to know that for the payment I request only secure pay, I prefer the payment to be done using eBay services. We will use a safe payment method because I am affiliated at eBay and I have a purchase protection account for $20,000.00 The final price that I want for this car is $2,980.00 including shipping and handling.

If you are interested in buying it please provide me your full name and address so I can initiate the deal through eBay.

I will wait your answer very soon.

Hello,

I am looking for caring and honest person to watch my 3 years old daughter while I work, during our stay in the state and a friend introduced craiglist.com to me, I was searching on Childcare Babysitter, when your Ad post pumped up as a Childcare and Babysitter, am interested in your service as my babysitter/Childcare.. My Little daughters is (Mellina) , I would like you to watch over her while i am at work in your Location , I reside in United Kingdom,I will be coming to the States in about two weeks time , Cos I just got a contract with Boss Perfume fashion industry down there, I work as a model and the contract will last for a month, the duration of our service wil be from 10am to 5pm, monday thru friday, I would like to know if she will be taken care of in your childcare centre/Home, or the hotel room where i would be lodging, It's Okay by me, any of this ways.

My little daughter (Mellina) is 3 years old, I will be waiting patiently for your email indicating the cost of everything,I mean the price for your service,how long you will be available to take care of her,how much u charge per week. she is just three years old as i have said earlier and i will be glad to update you and make the payment in advance to show you how serious i am. So please get back to me as soon as you can if you will be able to handle her and take very good care of her for me.

Email me back
Your's faithfully

> Thanks for your mail, since the cost of your bike is $800 i just contacted
my client about the cost of your bike and it present condition and he said
there is no problem about that.So my client said he will be issuing you a
Certified Check of $4000 while you wire 3000 to me through Western Union
Money Trasfer and you deduct the cost of your bike $800 and keep the
remaining $200 which my client said you should take for the terms of
Transaction and Agreement between you and my client.So i will like you to
send me your full contact information to where my client will be sending you
> the Certified Check like this;
> name........
> full address............
> city..............
> state............
> country.........
> zipcode...........
> cell/office/home phone number.........................
> I will look forward to the requested information as soon as possible to
that the check can be sent out to you immediately And do get back to me
with the Pics of the bike so tha! L my client will be Able to see What he
is paying off.Get back to me immediately. Looking torwards your
> respond,
> Best Regards.

Still have questions? try our help desk discussion forum or send us a note.

---

http://www.craigslist.org/about/scams   12/5/2010

Subj: **MTCN.....506 151 2419 PICK IT UP**
Date: 12/30/2010 7:14:59 P.M. Central Standard Time
From: osh4eva@yahoo.com
Reply-to: mr.edwardkelly@yahoo.com

PAYMENT NOTIFICATION

My dear I got your email and for you to be sure that I have sent the money you are advised to follow my instructions and track the MTCN

PAYMENT NOTIFICATION

GOOD DAY

I AM MR AUGUSTINE MATTEW OBUKOHWO THE MANAGER OF THE NIGERIAN WESTERN UNION HEARD OFFICE YOUR FUND WORTH $5HUNDRED THOUSAND UNITED STATES DOLLARS HAS BEEN DEPOSITED IN MY OFFICE FOR YOUR PAYMENT VIA WESTERN UNION WITH AN INSTRUCTION THAT ON NO ACCOUNT WILL I DEDUCT A DIAM OR TOUCH ANY THING FROM IT UNTIL IT IS SENT TO YOU FULLY NOW I HAVE JUST SENT THREE PAYMENT OF $5,000 TO YOU VIA WESTERN UNION

FIRST MAKE SURE YOU TRACK THE MONEY AND GO TO PICK IT UP

TRACK AND PICK UP/ www.westernunion.com
VIEW THIS LINK AND CLICK ON TRACKING www.westernunion.com

THEN FOLLOW THE DIRECTIONS AND FILL IN THE MTCN AND THE SENDERS NAME THEN CLICK ON CHECK STATUS AND YOU WILL SEE THAT IT IS VERY AVELABLE TO PICK UP BY YOU.

My brother I will advice you to be very fast in what ever you are doing so that you will pick up your money at once so I want you to make sure that you send the clearance fee today so that you can be able to pick up your fund before the end of today

YOUR FUND INFORMATION'S
- Hide quoted text -
SENDERS NAME : AUGUSTINE MATTEW. OBUKOHWO
MTCN................. 506 151 2419
TEXT ....Q. OK
ANSWER ....OK
AMOUNT SENT........................... $5,000.00

SENT FROM THE NEAREST COUNTRY REPUBLIC BENIN COTONOU.

2 ROLAND BERG SWEDEN
Senders Name AUGUSTINE MATTEW. OBUKOHWO
MTCN.....................308 256 9014
TEXT................... Q. OK
ANSWER ....OK

Friday, December 31, 2010 AOL: vicmanjlry

AMOUNT SENT...........$5,000.00

SENT FROM THE NEAREST COUNTRY REPUBLIC BENIN COTONOU.

3 STIG BERGLOF SWEDEN
SENDERS NAME : AUGUSTINE MATTEW. OBUKOHWO
MTCN................. 749 134 9444
TEXT ....Q. OK
ANSWER ....OK
AMOUNT SENT........$5,000.00

MONEY SENT FROM REPUBLIC BENIN COTONOU.

BUT NOTE THAT BEFORE YOU WILL BE ABLE TO PICK UP MONEY YOU NEED TO
PAY FOR CLEARANCE FEE WHICH WILL COST YOU $90 EACH , ONCE YOU
SEND THE MONEY ONLY THEN WILL YOU PICK UP THE 15,000

SEND THE $90 WITH BELOW IS WESTERN UNION OR MONEY GRAM INFORM ME
AT ONCE

Receivers name: NWAKOLO MOSES UTOMI

Receivers address Lagos Nigeria

Text question: when

Answer: today

ONCE YOU SEND THE MONEY YOU SHOULD SEND THE PAYMENT
INFORMATION INCLUDING THE (MTCN) NUMBER. AT ONCE FOR SO THAT
YOU'RE FUND WILL BE CLEARED TO PICKUP.

 NOTE THAT YOU JUST HAVE FROM NOW TILL TOMORROW TO GET THINGS
DONE.

I WAIT FOR YOUR URGENT REPLY

YOU'RE FAITHFULLY

AUGUSTINE MATTEW. OBUKOHWO

Friday, December 31, 2010 AOL: vicmanjlry

Subj: **STOP CONTACTING THOSE PEOPLE!!**
Date: 1/1/2011 6:10:54 P.M. Central Standard Time
From: office@barkerfinancial.com
Reply-to: dr.scotdaniel@windowslive.com
Attention: Beneficiary,

I am Mrs Lisa Jones, I am a US citizen, 48 years Old. I reside here in New Braunfels Texas. My residential address is as follows.108 Crockett Court. Apt 303, New Braunfels Texas, United States, am thinking of relocating since I am now rich. I am one of those that took part in the Compensation in Nigeria many years ago and they refused to pay me, I had paid over $20,000 while in the US, trying to get my payment all to no avail.

So I decided to travel down to Nigeria with all my compensation documents, And I was directed to meet Dr Scott Daniel , who is the member of COMPENSATION AWARD COMMITTEE, and I contacted him and he explained everything to me. He said whoever is contacting us through emails are fake.

He took me to the paying bank for the claim of my Compensation payment. Right now I am the most happiest woman on earth because I have received my compensation funds of $1,500,000.00. Moreover, Dr Scott Daniel, showed me the full information of those that are yet to receive their payments and I saw your name as one of the beneficiaries, and your email address, that is why I decided to email you to stop dealing with those people, they are not with your fund, they are only making money out of you. I will advise you to contact Dr Scott Daniel. You have to contact him directly on this information below.

JOAKIN COMPENSATION HOUSE
Name : Barrister Scott Daniel
Email: dr.scotdaniel@windowslive.com

You really have to stop dealing with those people that are contacting you and telling you that your fund is with them, it is not in anyway with them, they are only taking advantage of you and they will dry you up until you have nothing.

The only money I paid after I met Dr Scott Daniel was just $320 for the paper works, take note of that.Once again stop contacting those people, I will advise you to contact Dr Scott Daniel so that he can help you to Transfer your Fund into your account, instead of dealing with those liars that will be turning you around asking for different kind of money to complete your transaction.

Thank You and Be Blessed.

Mrs. Lisa Jones.

Saturday, January 01, 2011 AOL: VICMANJLRY

Subj: **URGENT MAIL**
Date: 12/27/2010 10:34:34 P.M. Central Standard Time
From: beatriz@tdomain.com
Reply-to: tuerphilipesq@gmail.com

You do not know me and neither do I know you. I am not desperate nor in need of help.I only want to be sure you are the kind of person I can trust with the following proposal.

I have been very careful in my selection and have taken pains to ensure I will be dealing with a person that has the intelligence to understand what I am getting myself into. From the little I have been able to deduce, I cannot make you agree to partner with me on this but I can assume that when you are in, I can trust you completely.

I am a UK based lawyer and I am bringing everything I have to the table; my reputation and all I have labored for my whole life.The least I ask of you, is for you, after hearing the proposal to honestly tell me if you are up for it or not, without acting maliciously. That way, I get to loose nothing and can walk away with my proposal and reputation intact without actually divulging full details.

I bear the full brunt of any risk involved in this business which I cannot do for your involvement. The thing is, anyone can serve but I chose you. I pray you don't let me down. For more details if interested by email(tuerphilipesq@gmail.com)

The fact of the proposal involves access to millions of Tax-Free United States Dollars. It is up to you to accept or decline. I am waiting to hear from you. Time is of the essence.

Yours faithfully,
Tuer Philip John Esq

Subj: **FROM: MRS. MANUELA JOHNSON,**
Date: 12/28/2010 1:24:47 P.M. Central Standard Time
From: eusecuritiesbv@netscape.net
Reply-to: agentservicebv@aim.com
ONLINE LOTTO AND GAMING CORPORATION
LAAN VAN HOORNWIJCK 55
2289 DG RIJSWIJK THE NETHERLANDS
WEBSITE: www.lotto.nl

MONTH OF DECEMBER ONLINE LOTTO AND GAMING CORPORATION.

WINNING NUMBER: OL/656/020/018

OUR DEAR WINNER,

THIS IS TO NOTIFY YOU THAT YOUR EMAIL ADDRESS HAS WON ONLINE LOTTO AND GAMING
CORPORATION SUM OF (ONE MILLION EURO), THIS ONLINE LOTTO AND GAMING
CORPORATION PROGRAM WAS MADE POSSIBLE BY GROUPS OF INTERNATIONAL COMPANIES
THAT DO ADVERTISEMENTS ON THE INTERNET TO APPRECIATE EMAIL USERS.

ALL THE E-MAIL ADDRESSES USED FOR THIS ONLINE LOTTO AND GAMING CORPORATION
PROGRAM WAS SELECTED THROUGH ELECTRONIC BALLOTING SYSTEM OF INTERNET E-MAIL
USERS, FROM WHICH YOUR E-MAIL ADDRESS CAME OUT AS THE WINNING COUPON.

WE THEREBY CONTACT YOU TO CLAIM YOUR WINNING AMOUNT QUICKLY AS THIS IS A
MONTHLY LOTTERY. FAILURE TO CLAIM YOUR WINNING WILL RESULT INTO THE REVERSION
OF OUR FOLLOWING MONTH LOTTERY. (THE EXPIRATION DATE IS 28TH OF JANUARY). PLEASE
CONTACT OUR APPROVED AGENT BELOW WITH YOUR WINNING NUMBER ABOVE.

ONLINE LOTTO AND GAMING CORPORATION AGENCY.
MRS. ANA PAULA FILIPE.
(DIRECTOR OF WINNING CLAIMS DEPARTMENT).
TEL: +31-620-669-926
E-MAIL: agentservicebv@aim.com

WARNING: YOU ARE TO KEEP EVERYTHING ABOUT THIS YOUR WINNING PRIVATE, UNTIL YOU
RECEIVE YOUR WINNING PRIZE BY THIS ONLINE LOTTO AND GAMING CORPORATION PAYING
BANK. CONTOVERSIAL CLAIM WILL LEAD TO DISQUALIFICATION. BE WARNED.

REGARDS,

MRS. MANUELA JOHNSON.
(DIRECTOR OF ONLINE LOTTO AND GAMING CORPORATION).

Tuesday, December 28, 2010 AOL: vicmanjlry

Subj: **Re: UN-005-JJ5**
Date: 12/30/2010 4:58:42 A.M. Central Standard Time
From: mrshillaryclintonoffice1@mail.mn
To: VICMANJLRY@aol.com

Dear: E. A. Rooney

Deliver Process

I am promising you that everything will be fine, all you just need is follow the instruction giving to you by United Nations Boad, so you can get your ATM CARD, i want you to know that you are not going to pay any fee, Only delivery fee of your ATM CARD to your Destination address by the UPS.

Confirmation,however, the awareness of the United Nations signify a prove that you have been approved by the United a fast process on your compensation fund.

Upon the Approval Document that we have received from the United Nations Board on your behalf to ensure that a valid facilitation process of installation of your fund into the fast payment method which is signified as a inter Switch ATM Card payment.

Due to the rules and regulation of the United Nations Board Committees we want you to know that this Bank will put a perfect payment to your transaction to enable us meet up with the given date that has been instructed by the United Nations Committees, all we need from you is your response and regular attention to any mails you might received from us to enable you receive your ATM Card immediately from Courier Service that has been registered by the United Nation Board Committees to safe guard your delivery to your home address after the successful
process of your Card.

We are not going to call you on phone only by email. However, upon that the rules and regulation and procedures of this Bank, we will like to keep you informed that your ATM Card will be as soon as you send your Details.

2: Full contact address.................
city...................
state.............
zip-code........ country.........

3: Age..........................

Thursday, December 30, 2010 AOL: vicmanjlry

...
4: E-mail ....
6: What is your Annual Income ? ....
7: Name of Bank: ....
Occupation ....

9: A COPY OF YOUR INTERNATIONAL PASSPORT ....

Kindly get Back to us as soon as you have receive this email by telling us that you have confirmed our email to enable us act accordingly to your response and be informed that we don't want Rude message from you and don't be greedy

I await your anticipated response.

Mrs. Hillary Clinton

On Wed, Dec 29, 2010 at 9:51 PM, <VICMANJLRY@aol.com> wrote:
To Whom it MAY Concern:
Pease send my payment ATM card to:
E. A. Rooney 7842 Rollingbrook Drive
Houston, Texas 77071
Sincerely,
E. A. Rooney

In a message dated 12/29/2010 5:19:01 A.M. Central Standard Time, mrshillaryclintonoffice1@mail.mn writes:

UNITED NATIONS (UNITED NATIONS ASSISTED PROGRAM)

DIRECTORATE OF INTERNATIONAL PAYMENT AND TRANSFERS. UNITED NATIONS LIAISON OFFICE http://www.un.org The Sum of $500,000.00 US D Only

COMPENSATION UNIT, IN AFFILIATION WITH THE UNITED NATION. Send a copy of your response to Secretary of the state

Strictly Attn: Beneficiary.

Good day, from our records here we find out that up till this very moment you have not received your Compensation Payment.

We have been having a meeting for the passed 7 months which ended 2 days ago with the secretary Mrs Hillary Clinton to the UNITED NATIONS. This email is to all the people that have been scammed in any part of the world.

This includes every foreign contractors that may have not received their contract sum,and people that have had an unfinished transaction or international businesses that failed due to Government problems etc.

We found your name in our list and that is why we are contacting you,This have been agreed upon and have been signed Therefore,we are happy to inform you that an arrangement has perfectly been concluded to effect your payment as soon as possible in our bid to be transparent.

Thursday, December 30, 2010 AOL: vicmanjlry

You are hereby advice to stop further communication with any person or Office regards to these and do take immediate contact with Dr. Mrs. Hillary Clinton of Oceanic Bank London for immediate release of your Compensation Payment by ATM CARD. Oceanic Bank is the only authorized Bank we are operating with as we are in partnership with the Bank, if you get any mail from any other Banks regards to these please disregard it to avoid Scam.

You have 7 working days to do these or forget all about it. Adhere with the advice given to you by her as she is our Representative over there.If in any way this message did not related to you, please do not take any further step.

Your payment File Number UN-005-JJ5, give it to her during the event of your contact with her. Secretary of the State Mrs Hillary Clinton Contact Email :

mrshillaryclintonoffice1@mail.mn

Making the world a better place for all.
With Kind Regards,
Ban Ki-Moon

UN Secretary-General
http://www.un.org/sg

Signature Over Printed Name: _____

Date: _____

Feel free to send your comments about the marketing process along with this form. We welcome your feedback!

Thursday, December 30, 2010 AOL: vicmanjlry

Subj: **Time of Switzerland SA - Job Offer**
Date: 11/17/2010 2:40:04 P.M. Central Standard Time
From: time@users.com
Dear valued friend,

Our company, **Time of Switzerland SA**, is offering part-time jobs as a finance officer in the United States.

What tasks you have as a finance officer:

- Receive payments from our customers via Bank Transfers;
- 10% of the payment amount will be your commission;
- The rest of 90% of the payment will be sent to one of our offices in Europe;

What incomes you have as a finance officer:

- Your incomes will depend on the orders we have in your area per week;
e.g. If you process a 4,000USD order your income will be 400USD

To enroll for this job click the following link and you will be redirected to our application form:
Click here to go to the application form

After you have submitted the application form, you will be contacted by our Human Resource Department within 24 hours to schedule the first payments.

Adele D. Barrens,
Human Resource Assistant Manager,
Time of Switzerland SA.

Wednesday, December 08, 2010 AOL: vicmanjlry

Subj: **Re: Business Proposition-Please reply**
Date: 12/6/2010 8:34:50 A.M. Central Standard Time
From: grace.ramoutar@santander.com
Reply-to: mrsd_operations@mail.mn

6th of December 2010.

Hello,

My name is Mrs.Grace Ramoutar, a Canadian citizen working for Santander Bank in London and I am sending you this mail from my office through the internet with reservations. Please do reply to my private email (mrsd_operations@mail.mn) for security reasons. Basically the issue I want to unravel to you is very classified and confidential but it involves a huge sum of money(Ten Million Five Hundred Thousand United States Dollars) from a foreign deceased customer, Hans Douglas, deposited here in the Bank where I work. The choice of contacting you is aroused from the geographical nature of where you live, particularly due to the sensitivity of the transaction and the confidentiality herein. However, I would like to seek your permission to have you stand as the family representative of the deceased to retrieve the funds into your account.

Please I need your urgent co-operation because I do not want the bank to label the account as unserviceable at the end of the year final audit which comes 31 December so that's why I need your assistance. I know this business will be of immense benefit to you, as I am privy to all Information that will be use to facilitate the release of the funds to you. If you are willing to accept my proposal kindly reply my mail with your full name, address and phone/fax number, by indicating your interest, thereafter percentages and more information will be relayed to you on my next mail.

Sincerely Yours,

Mrs. Grace Ramoutar
Santander Bank
406 Strand, London, WC2RUNE
www.santander.com

Thursday, December 09, 2010 AOL: vicmanjlry

Subj: **FUNDS READY FOR TRANSFER**
Date: 12/9/2010 9:13:12 A.M. Central Standard Time
From: anne.behotas t@ac-rouen.fr
Reply-to.   balanorgan@hotmail.com

THE WILL HAS BEEN EXECUTED
Barristers' Chambers
ALAN ORGAN & ASSOCIATES
Address:33, Bedford Row
London WC1R 4JH, England
LONDON - UK.

Attention:Client,

On behalf of the Trustees and Executor of the estate of Late Eng.Gregory
Rims. I once again try to notify you as my earlier letter was returned
undelivered. I hereby attempt to reach you again by this same email
address on the WILL. I wish to notify you that late Gregory Rims made
you a beneficiary in his WILL. He left the sum of Thirty Million Dollars
(USD$30,000.000.00) to you in the Codicil and last testament to his WILL.

This may sound strange and unbelievable to you, but it is real and true.
Being a widely traveled man, he said he met you sometime in past or
simply you were nominated to him by one of his numerous friends abroad who
wished you good, I am not too sure again. Gregory Rims until his death
was a member of the Helicopter Society and the Institute of Electronic &
Electrical Engineers and a German property magnate. He was a very
dedicated Christian who loved to give out alms to the poor,hungry and
needy. His great philanthropy earned him numerous awards during his life
time. Late Gregory Rims died on the 13th day of December,2004 at the
age of 80 years, and his WILL is now ready for execution after 3 years and
thorough investigations.

According to him, this money is to support your humanitarian/medical
activities and to help the poor and the needy in our society. Please if I
reach you as I am hopeful, endeavor to get back to me as soon as possible
to enable me conclude my job. I hope to hear from you in no distant time.
I await your prompt response and please keep this very discrete and to
yourself until the transfer of the funds to you is finalized.
Yours in Service,
Barrister Alan Organ.

Thursday, December 09, 2010 AOL: vicmanjlry

Subj: **are you looking for a girl?**
Date: 12/7/2010 1:15:43 A.M. Central Standard Time
From: anniesmith9072047@yahoo.com
To: axluqrykqeooiv@hotmail.com
    http://6819.luvtaburlgfz.in/

Wednesday, December 08, 2010 AOL: vicmanjlry

```
Subj:     what are you looking for?
Date:     12/7/2010 11:39:06 P.M. Central Standard Time
From:     bonniehenderson3776511@yahoo.com
To:       dhkiyedrljhebs@hotmail.com
  http://6341.wxaeceitfsvo.in/
```

Wednesday, December 08, 2010 AOL: vicmanjlry

This Is A pharmacy scam
Much of the medicine from China and India is counterfeit-not real .
NEVER buy medicine over the Internet

In a message dated 12/7/2010 11:09:34 A.M. Central Standard Time, hwadam328762@aol.com writes:

yPHARMACYk
http://www.grupo-sph.com/t10.html

Wednesday, December 08, 2010 AOL: vicmanjlry

Subj: **You could get paid for your time**
Date: 12/4/2010 9:09:21 A.M. Central Standard Time
From: lucy@liquorinthebox.info
Reply-to: Tarikanxknpp@liquorinthebox.info
To: vicmanjlry@aol.com

H=O=T O=F=F=E-R=S   F=O-R   T-O-D-A=Y
ISSUE #91658034

URGENT NEWS: You can make up to $75 for each survey taken.

Here is a outstanding survey panel seeking panelists. Simply share your opinion
on a bunch of topics. Product developers are willing to pay reviewers between
$5 and $75 per completed survey. Join up below, free.
http://bhjh.liquorinthebox.info/lzj/gbe/enw/noese/dlng/

Product reviewing
Take simple online surveys
Keep the products you review
Get cash for your thoughts
http://bhjh.liquorinthebox.info/lzj/gbe/enw/noese/dlng/

All you've examined above is an advert.

http://bdjh.liquorinthebox.info/lnfwbofz/wnoope/hvzc/
Or Contact
2-4-3 Fifth Ave.

Wednesday, December 08, 2010 AOL: vicmanjlry

Subj: **Longest time Master!!!**
Date: 11/20/2010 10:10:50 A.M. Central Standard Time
From: slavemarryquin@yahoo.com
To: VICMANJLRY@aol.com

Good morning and how are you doing Sir,Sir i have been waiting for you to write since when you have told me you will add me to your list but since then i did not get back from you that is why i try to check you may be you are still okay and ready to owned me and relocate me to be with you and serve you with all my heart.Sir i hope you are still in searching of a slave who is going to be with you and belong to you for ever and ever because i am still also looking for a master who is going to owned me and take good care of me while i also take good care of his house all the time when he is at home or not to make him happy all the time when i am with him living there till the rest of my life eternity life.Sir i am waiting to hear back from you asap you get my email.
Thank's
Your sexy Slave

Wednesday, December 08, 2010 AOL: vicmanjlry

Subj: **Re: SARAFINA .**
Date: 11/13/2010 7:32:39 P.M. Central Standard Time
From: jsara111@yahoo.com
To: VICMANJLRY@aol.com

Dearest Gene, thanks for sharing your time with me !I love what i have been reading about you and thanks for sharing your time in writing me personally on here as well,I read and understand what you wrote..I want you to know that i am a one woman and i hope you are the same , i want to face you only..I have been hurt in the past relationship and I dont want to get hurt anymore! so this is why i have single ,in no rush searching for the right man ! I am very attracted to you and i am glad becos we have many good things in common

I will try and tell you more about myself as we know our selves better Im a loving,kind,honest , truthful and very caring woman and I like reading cooking sports travelling and biking writing poems...i also love kids and pets! I have never been married !
My dad is an american indian while my mom is from asian african .I live with my mom now,i love my mom so much,i can do anything for her to make her happy and she loves me too ... my dad is late ! Many years ago my dad came down to africa and took me and mom along with him to california
My mom is 60yrs old and I am the only sibling of my parents. .After the death of my dad when things are not going too well for me and my mother my mom decided to relocate back to africa,Here i schooled and studied nursing,I would love to come start up a new life with the right man anywhere in the world!!
Well i believe distance,age,beauty,colour,race is nothing and not a problem in a relationship..for its the love,honesty and care two have for each other matters most...I hope we will find we have many common goals and interests that will make us at least good friends which is the first step in reaching a stronger and lifelasting relationship....
As I am tired of being single.I search for that one special an to call my other completion of a whole life ..I am just glad we found eachother on the site and i am very interested in you !I so much hope you the right man i have been searching for , for me to share the restof my life with Have good home and i really hope we can be more than friends. Please tell me more about yourself if there is ? as well thanks and send me more of your pictures !

please take good care of yourself for me
Sarafina

Hello my dear Gene, How are you doing? thanks for writing me on the site .
I am so glad to finally have the opportunity to learn more about you and outlook on life in
general and your personal interest and desires in particular.
I am surprise that some lucky woman has not captured your heart, but I am also glad that they
have not at the same time as it will give me the opportunity to become more then friends if we
develope that type of relationship, I am new on here really looking to love and beloved.. when
did you joined the site, have you talked to someone on there before ? what are the type of
woman you have talked to ? where are they from? .

I want you to tell me more about yourself what do you do for fun; your work, family and social
life; what you do for entertainment and things like that; I also want you to send me some
pictures of yourself that you think that I would like. On that note I will close and I look forward
to your timely reply.Please take good care of yourself for me and write back soon.. I also have
yahoo messenger chat   do you have? you can download it here www.messenger.yahoo.com
Sarafina

Wednesday, December 08, 2010 AOL: vicmanjlry

About the Author

I was born in Brooklyn, New York and lived on Long Island until I was nine years old. My mother remarried and moved to Florida in nineteen fifty. Unknown to me at this time, I brought the polio virus to Florida from Long Island and got polio on my right side of my body. I was in the West Palm Beach Florida hospital for about six months. I was suppose to die or never walk again, but this never happened. I did walk out of the hospital without a brace or needing a wheel chair God had other plans for me in life.

My mother met a physic in the last sixties and was told I was suppose to die but was spared to accomplish many things in this World. Writing this book is one of them

I have had an interesting life. After serving in the US Air Force, passing the physical, and was discharge in nineteen sixty three and I work on project Fire for RCA, Ascension Island, man on the Moon project. I made numerous trips to Recife, Brazil. where I attended many Voodoo functions. I then went to Florida State University and earned a degree in Geography. in nineteen sixty eight. I was recruited by the Defense Intelligence Agency as analyst. This was not for me and went into my hobby in jewelry as a Graduate Gemologist. I worked in jewelry for over thirty years and understand the American banking system. I have always been creative. I moved to Houston, Texas after my wife died of cancer on the advise of a friend. He told me when I get too old he would put in a Jewish home in Houston. I took a writing course from Long Ridge Writers Group, which helped me write this book

I have been evolved in Internet scams since nineteen ninety nine. During this time I have traveled three times to Vietnam, two times to China for love which never happened.

I also traveled to Thailand, Cambodia, Russia, Budapest, Hungary

Due to my World travels, in business for over thirty years, I know about the American Banking system, Wiring money to any place in the World and know how scams work. Buying this book will save you hundreds or thousands of dollars. Take Care, God bless.

For comments and Suggestions you may email

the author at vicmanjlry@aol.com.